Let's Huddle

friends, faith and fun at the table

Sherri DeWalt

WestBow Press books may be ordered through booksellers or by contacting:

WestBow Press
A Division of Thomas Nelson & Zondervan
1663 Liberty Drive
Bloomington, IN 47403
www.westbowpress.com
844-714-3454

ISBN: 979-8-3850-3103-0 (sc)
ISBN: 979-8-3850-3104-7 (hc)
ISBN: 979-8-3850-3105-4 (e)

Library of Congress Control Number: 2024916095

Print information available on the last page.

WestBow Press rev. date: 09/25/2024

WESTBOW
PRESS®
A DIVISION OF THOMAS NELSON
& ZONDERVAN

To all women who desire to serve the Lord and make Him known.
And to three of my greatest loves, Jay, Ryan, and Isabel.

Contents

"This is my commandment that you love one another as I have loved you."

—John 15:12

Preface

In 2019, I invited several friends and acquaintances to be part of a small group called a *huddle*. We began meeting in my home twice a month to share a meal, have meaningful conversations, and have fun. The group quickly bonded and flourished because of the real need in our lives for connection, investment in friendship, creativity, opportunities to serve, and the importance of introducing and pointing others toward God and His Word. More huddles formed. Life-giving and sustaining friendships are growing. The gospel is spreading.

Introduction

Lives are changed at the table. Talking, creating, laughing, and eating with friends in your home is a bold form of love. Jesus was often found eating with others, serving food, telling stories, and asking questions. Opening your heart and home to nurture relationships and point to Christ has eternal value.

People need meaningful friendships and connections with others, and the greatest need of every person is to know God. Mother Teresa said,

> I find the poverty of the West, much, much, much greater, much more difficult to remove because a piece of bread will not satisfy the hunger of the heart. The hunger for love is much more difficult to remove than the hunger for bread. There is a great hunger for God in the world today.

Hospitality involves a commitment of time, energy, and resources. Building relationships requires intentionality and planning. Pouring yourself out to love and serve others is a life-giving and noble choice; you are never alone. Before He ascended into heaven, Jesus told His disciples to proclaim the gospel to all people, and He would be with them always.

This book provides a road map for you to create a seed-scattering ministry of hospitality. It contains content for two six-session series, as well as ideas for holidays and special events. Depending on when you launch your group, you may want to add a holiday huddle, charity huddle, or excursion to the schedule.

Anakeimai is Greek for "at the table."
The gospels contain nine accounts of Jesus *at the table*.

Getting Started

Just start. A warm welcome and wild curiosity about others creates the perfect setting for relationships to grow and people to feel known. These ever-increasing friendships will bless your life in immeasurable ways. Don't wait until your home, life, or schedule is perfect.

Partner. Launching your group with a friend will make it more enjoyable and sustainable.

Pray. Ask the Lord to lead you regarding whom to invite. You may be surprised by the way the group forms. Continue to pray regularly for each person who joins your group.

Invite. Several weeks before your first meeting, extend invitations. Aim for the number of people who can squeeze around a large table.

Whether you call, text, email, or put something in the mail, your invitation should specifically indicate the dates/times you plan to meet. Meetings usually last one and a half to two hours. Sample language follows:

Let's Huddle!

Please join us to strengthen friendship and faith
through creative projects, fun, and conversations.

Food. Keep the food simple. A big pot of oatmeal, soup, or salad is perfect. Improvisational "no-recipe" recipes are included for those who would like some ideas.

Materials. Besides gathering small gifts and the craft supplies you will need, you may want to visit a local thrift store to collect pretty bowls, plates, and utensils you reserve for your group to make hosting easy.

Make it your own. Be creative and flexible, modifying the content to meet your group's interests, needs, and personality.

Book Recommendation

Rosaria Butterfield came to Christ through the love and hospitality of her neighbors. In her book, *The Gospel Comes with a House Key*, she explains how she starts the day with a big pot of something to share on the stove. Her home is a beehive of constant activity and guests.

God called Nehemiah to rebuild the wall around Jerusalem. Many people rose to help, often repairing the wall section closest to their homes. Analogously, in our broken world, we can each begin the repair and healing process by being a source of light and love to those close to our homes.

First Series—Beauty

Air plants are an inexpensive but meaningful gift and
can be purchased in multipacks online.

Beauty

Fun

Give everyone a small welcome gift to set the tone for fun. A few pieces of candy gathered up
in brightly colored tissue paper tied with a ribbon, small plants, or dollar store seasonal items
all make great gifts.

Warmly welcome and introduce all guests to one another. Share why you started the group as well as upcoming dates, topics, and projects.

Pair Game

1. Distribute pens and paper.
2. Divide the group into pairs.
3. Set a timer for ten minutes.
4. See which pair can come up with the most things in common.

Known and Heard

- ♦ What would you want it to be if rain could fall in any scent?
- ♦ Where would you choose if you could float in a hot-air balloon over any city or place in the world?
- ♦ What is your favorite time of the day?

- • Collect contact information, including cell phone numbers, email addresses, and birthdates, and share with the group before the next meeting.
- • Note each person's birthday in your calendar so you can send a text or card.
- • Use name tags for the first couple of meetings until everyone knows one another's names.

Beauty

Seeing and celebrating beauty heals our souls and opens our hearts and minds to live with more meaning, purpose, and joy. Beauty is all around us, in the natural world, art, music, people, and even difficult circumstances.

Discussion Blueprint

- • *Shinrin-yoku.* The Japanese have a form of nature therapy called *Shinrin-yoku.* The term was coined in 1982 and translates as "forest bathing." It is simply spending time outside in nature and observing (for example, going for a slow walk in a park or even your neighborhood and paying attention to what you see, hear, and smell). Forest bathing has documented positive physical and psychological effects, from improving the immune, cardiovascular, and respiratory function to reducing depression, anxiety, and anger.[1]

- *Awe.* Like curiosity, surprise, and wonder, new experiences activate awe. We are filled with awe when we experience something vast or remarkable beyond our regular experience and frame of reference. Research strongly suggests experiencing awe is a fast track to personal change and growth. It can make you happier, healthier, humble, generous, and connected to the people around you. It also may help you think more critically, decrease materialism, and make you feel you have more time.[2] Experiencing awe reorients us to God's majesty and our place in relationship to Him and others.

- *Beauty in the difficult.* With increasing global conflict, it can be difficult to reconcile a beauty-first approach with violence, war, and suffering. We must expand our definition of beauty beyond the beauty of nature and obvious good things and seek to find and act in beautiful ways to defy forces of evil, disorder, and destruction. Under challenging circumstances, look for opportunities to offer presence and support, facilitate healing, provide resources, and pray.

- Consider one or more of the following quotes/verses:

> We no longer dare to believe in beauty, and we make of it a mere appearance in order the more easily to dispose of it. Our situation today shows that beauty demands for itself at least as much courage and decision as do truth and goodness, and she will not allow herself to be separated and banned from her two sisters without taking them along with herself in an act of mysterious vengeance. We can be sure that whoever sneers at her name as if she were the ornament of a bourgeois past—whether he admits it or not—can no longer pray and soon will no longer be able to love. (Hans Urs von Balthasar[3])

> The heavens declare the glory of God, and the sky above proclaims his handiwork. Day to day pours out speech, and night to night reveals knowledge. There is no speech, nor are there words, whose voice is not heard. Their voice goes out through all the earth, and their words to the end of the world. In

them he has set a tent for the sun, which comes out like a bridegroom leaving his chamber, and, like a strong man, runs its course with joy. Its rising is from the end of the heavens, and its circuit to the end of them, and there is nothing hidden from its heat. (Psalm 19:1–6)

Finally, brothers, whatever is true, whatever is honorable, whatever is just, whatever is pure, whatever is lovely, whatever is commendable, if there is any excellence, if there is anything worthy of praise, think about these things. (Philippians 4:8)

Known and Loved

- ♦ What most inspires awe in you? (Many of the answers may involve the beauty of nature or the miracle of life. Something deep down in our souls recognizes our humble place in the universe.)
- ♦ How can we incorporate rhythms of beauty into our lives?
- ♦ How can we expand our definition of beauty?
- ♦ Is beauty a luxury for the affluent?

Beyond the Table

- Try practicing Shinrin-yoku. Spend time outside and observe closely what you see. Breathe the air in fully and slowly. What do you smell? Touch a tree or flower. Listen to the animals and the wind.
- Describe what you see, hear, smell, and touch in a journal or note to yourself.
- Collect at least five different types of fallen leaves. Bring them inside your home to display or flatten them in the back of a book.

Gratitude

Fun

Thankful Game

Designate a place on each side of the room, read from the list below, and ask people to gather according to which of the two they are most grateful for or most enjoy. If space does not permit, ask for a show of hands.

- dogs/cats
- warm fire / crisp walk
- chocolate/vanilla
- beach/mountains
- books/movies
- banana split / charcuterie board
- crockpot/restaurant

- ◆ Name a simple, everyday joy.
- ◆ Is there an event or opportunity that you are looking forward to?
- ◆ What is an advancement in technology that has significantly improved your life?

Gratitude

Consciously living with more gratitude will profoundly affect how we experience the world and our ability to influence it for good. People characterized by gratitude are measurably happier, more peaceful, and more uplifting to those around them. It is God's desire for us to be grateful! We can grow in gratitude.

Discussion Blueprint

View five-minute film. The short film *Gratitude* inspires us to view each day with fresh eyes, savor the beauty in others, and cherish the miracle of everyday life. It includes a meditation written and read by Benedictine monk Brother David Steindl-Rast, set to music by award-winning composer Gary Matlin, and filmed by Louie Schwartzberg. Viewed by millions worldwide, you can find it on YouTube and the Grateful Living website.

Discuss film.

- • How did this film make you feel?
- • What did you find most powerful?

Gratitude changes your brain. Simply expressing gratitude has a lasting effect on your brain. In a study published by the University of California, Berkley, in 2017,[4] three hundred adults who were seeking mental health counseling for depression and anxiety were assigned randomly to three groups. The first group was instructed to write one gratitude letter to another person each week for three weeks. The second group was asked to write their deepest thoughts and feelings about negative experiences. The third group had no writing activity. All the participants received counseling. The study found that those who wrote gratitude letters experienced significantly better mental health four weeks and twelve weeks after their writing exercise ended compared to both other groups. Brain scans showed significantly greater activation in the medial prefrontal cortex of the gratitude letter writers. Interestingly, the positive effect did not emerge immediately but gradually over several weeks and was even greater after three months. The researchers concluded that writing the gratitude letters resulted in such a positive outcome because it shifted the participants' attention away from negative emotions.

It is God's will for us to be grateful. Consider the following verses:

> Rejoice always, pray without ceasing, give thanks in all circumstances, for this is the will of God in Christ Jesus for you. (1 Thessalonians 5:16–18)

> Do not be anxious about anything, but in everything by prayer and supplication with thanksgiving let your requests be made known to God. And the peace of God which surpasses understanding will guard your heart. (Philippians 4:6)

Many people are searching for God's will for their lives and may be surprised to learn that gratitude and prayer are not only part of God's will for us but also part of God's remedy for anxiety.

Known and Loved

- ◆ Who has most positively influenced your life, and what are you most grateful to them for?
- ◆ How can you incorporate gratitude when praying about your anxieties?
- ◆ What do you wish you would never have to worry about again? Why?

Beyond the Table

- Before falling asleep each night, experiment with thinking of five things you are grateful for from the day.
- Tie a brightly colored thread or ribbon around your wrist to remind yourself to be thankful throughout the day.
- Send a card or note to someone expressing your appreciation and gratitude for them.
- Memorize Philippians 4:6.

Book Recommendation

In her book *One Thousand Gifts*, Ann Voskamp, a self-described farmer's wife and mother, challenged herself to write a list of one thousand things for which she is grateful. Her beautiful, sometimes whimsical list includes the following:

- morning shadows across the old floors
- jam piled high on toast
- leafy life scent of the florist shop
- wind flying cold and wild in hair

Terrariums

Fun

Questions in a Bowl

Copy the questions, cut them apart, fold them, and place them in a bowl. Allow each person to draw a question from the bowl, answer it, and return it to the bowl.

- — What emoji do you use most frequently?
- — What was the worst haircut you ever had in your life?
- — Who was your childhood famous-person crush?
- — Have you ever been told you resemble someone famous? If so, who?
- — If you could bring back any fashion trend, which would you get back?
- — Does your car (or any previous car you owned) have a name? What is/was it?

Terrarium

Design and arrange a miniature ecosystem using plants, soil, rocks, and decorative elements. Making terrariums together releases creativity, provides relaxation, and fosters a deeper connection to nature and each other.

- open or closed glass containers of different shapes and sizes
- potting soil
- small plants and mosses
- gravel or crushed stones for the drainage layer
- miniature figures, pebbles, and other items to add interest

1. Place a two-inch layer of gravel in the bottom of a glass container to promote drainage.
2. Fill with potting soil up to two inches from the rim.
3. Add plants and decorations.

Thrift, secondhand, and dollar stores are great places to hunt for fun containers and small items to decorate terrariums. Mosses often grow in moist, shady areas, particularly under trees. Choose slow-growing plants that thrive in low to medium light; great options include African violet, creeping fig, club moss, pothos, small ferns, lucky bamboo and prayer, nerve, and polka dot plants. Succulents and cacti can also be used but work best in open containers. Ask your huddle friends to bring containers and help collect the needed supplies.

Table Talk

- ◆ Describe your last experience enjoying nature.
- ◆ What would it be like if you were entirely in charge of heaven?
- ◆ Share about a situation in your life that occupies your heart and mind.

The Dance by Edgar Degas, courtesy of National Gallery of Art's collection dataset

Celebrating the Arts

Fun

Place stickers under two plates and give prizes to people with stickers under their plates. Dish towels, bath products, and seasonal decor make great prizes.

Known and Heard

- ♦ What is the last song you heard that you enjoyed? Why?
- ♦ Do you prefer modern or traditional art?
- ♦ What is your favorite book or genre of literature?

Celebrating the Arts

Poetry, art, literature, and music can enrich our lives by stimulating our imagination, introducing us to new perspectives, helping us experience and process emotions, and fostering a sense of shared humanity. They invite us to engage in deeper reflection, critical thinking, and personal growth.

Discussion Blueprint

Exploring Music

Wolfgang Amadeus Mozart was born in Austria in 1756 and died in 1791 at age thirty-five. He was one of the greatest composers in the history of Western music, composing more than eight hundred works.

Listen to Mozart's Requiem "Lux Aeterna" together.

Requiem is a mass for the souls of the dead. *Lux Astern* means eternal light.

- How would you describe the tone or the mood?
- Did any instrument(s) stand out?
- Did the music bring any image to your mind?

Exploring Poetry

William Blake was an English poet, painter, and printmaker who lived from 1757 to 1827. Eccentric in life and dying in poverty, he has since become a seminal figure of the Romantic Age.

Pass out copies of the excerpt (or screenshot) from the poem "Auguries of Innocence" by William Blake:

> To see a world in a grain of sand.
> And a Heaven in a Wild Flower
> Hold Infinity in the palm of your hand
> And Eternity in an Hour [5]

Allow a few moments for silent reading. Ask for a volunteer to read the poem aloud.

– Which lines jump out to you?
– How does it make you feel?
– What do you think the message is?

Observing Art

Edgar Degas was a French impressionist. He was born in 1834 and died in 1917. The oldest of five children, his mother died when he was thirteen. More than half of his works depict dancers. Unlike many Impressionists, he always painted indoors, from memory, photographs, or live models.

Pass out copies (or screenshot) of *The Dance Class* by Edgar Degas. Allow a few minutes for observation and then discuss.

– Describe the scene in detail. What do you notice?
– What stories does the painting tell?
– How does this painting make you feel? Does it evoke memories or desires?
– Why do you think his pictures of ballerinas were and are so popular?

> *Conversation Art Cards,* created by Jane Fox, highlight twenty-five works of art and provide discussion question on topics ranging from vulnerability, people pleasing, fear, rest, hate, happiness, generosity, beauty, creativity, grief, and friendship.[6]

Known and Loved

♦ What would you try if you knew you couldn't fail?
♦ What is one thing you are not currently doing that, if you started to do it, would make a significant and positive impact on your life?

- Visit an art museum or go to a concert with a friend.
- Write a haiku celebrating the beauty of creation and the Creator. A haiku is a short poem containing three lines. This form of poetry originated in Japan. The first has five syllables, the second has seven, and the third has five. Traditionally, haikus are about nature, and they don't rhyme.

Acupressure rings

Imago Dei

Fun

Treat your friends to acupressure rings. Rolling them stimulates reflexology zones on the hands and fingers to relieve fatigue, boost energy, and aid concentration. They are inexpensive and can be purchased in multipacks online.

Known and Heard

- ♦ What is your favorite practice or product to reduce stress?
- ♦ Share one good thing that happened in the last week.
- ♦ Where have you recently discovered beauty in an unexpected place?

Imago Dei

God makes every person in His image. This remarkable and foundational truth impacts everything. Humans possess rationality, imagination, and moral agency. We are designed for relationships, to love and be loved. We can create and delight in beauty. All people are God's image bearers and should be valued, respected, and protected. As we seek to know God better, we will better reflect His image.

The Creation of Adam by Michelangelo

Discussion Blueprint

The Creation of Adam was painted by Michelangelo in 1511 on the ceiling of the Sistine Chapel in the Vatican in Rome, Italy. It is one of the most iconic paintings in the world. *The Creation of Adam* took sixteen days to complete. Michelangelo was inspired by the creation account in Genesis 1:26; God said, "Let us make man in our image, after our likeness." The "our" in the verse refers to the trinity—Father, Son, and Holy Ghost. Share a copy or screenshot of the picture with the group. Allow a few minutes for observation and discuss.

– Compare the facial expressions, posture, and actions of God and Adam.

God is all-powerful, all knowing, present everywhere, nonchanging, and perfectly holy. He alone possesses these attributes, and we can take great comfort in being made by such a powerful, perfect God. God is also just, loving, merciful, and faithful; we can seek to grow to be more like Him in these ways. People are often not treated as image bearers of God. Some extreme examples include children sold into sex slavery, mentally ill people who are homeless and ignored, unjust wars, and violence. Conversely, examples of people acting as image bearers of God are a patient mother who tenderly cares for her children, an artist painting, and a friend helping others to resolve conflict. Every day, opportunities confront us to reflect on God's image and treat others as image bearers. As image bearers, we should reflect God's image. So it's vital that we know God and have an accurate picture of Him. Our image of God may be skewed, incomplete, or inaccurate. Our upbringing, culture, and experiences can impact and limit our view of God. In reality, God is multidimensional, perfect in love and justice. A. W. Tozer famously said, "What comes into our minds when we think about God is the most important thing about us."[7]

Discuss the following:

– What comes into your mind when you think about God?
– How can reflecting on the fact that you and others bear the image of God impact your daily life?

How to learn more about the image of God. The Bible is the best book to study to understand God better. Jesus is 100 percent God and 100 percent human, so we can look to Him to learn about God and as a role model.

Look at a short passage together. Give everyone a copy of Luke 7:11–15, pen, and paper.

> Soon afterward, he went to a town called Nain, and his disciples and a great crowd went with him. As he drew near to the gate of the city, behold, a man

who had died was being carried out, the only son of his mother, and she was a widow, and a considerable crowd from the town was with her. And when the Lord saw her, he had compassion on her and said to her, "Do not weep." Then he came up and touched the bier, and the bearers stood still. And he said, "Young man, I say to you, arise." And the dead man sat up and began to speak, and Jesus gave him to his mother. (Luke 7:11–15)

Ask everyone to list basic observations about Jesus and His actions from the passage.

Examples follow:

- People followed Him.
- He saw the widow.
- He had compassion for her.
- He told her not to cry.
- He drew near to the bier and touched it.
- He told the young man to "arise."
- He gave him to his mother.

What conclusions can we draw about Jesus?

Suggestions follow:

- Despite everyone around, He focused on the mom's heartache.
- He was moved to compassion and acted.
- He understands the pain of a mother's loss of her son.
- His actions impacted people; He touched the bier, and the bearers stood still; He told the young man to arise, and he did!

What can we learn from Jesus?

Known and Loved

- What person, practice, or experience most shaped your knowledge and understanding of God?
- How have you grown in your knowledge and understanding of God, or how has it changed over the years?
- Do you desire to grow in your knowledge and understanding of God, and if so, what steps could you take?

Beyond the Table

Prayerfully consider how you might help someone who is suffering and act.

> Therefore be imitators of God as beloved children. And walk in love, as Christ loved us and gave himself up for us, a fragrant offering and sacrifice to God. (Ephesians 5:1–2)

Kintsugi

Fun

Questions in a Bowl

Copy the questions, cut them apart, fold them, and place them in a bowl. Allow each person to draw a question from the bowl, answer it, and return it to the bowl.

- What song do you pick when singing karaoke?
- Do you still hate your least favorite food as a child? What was it?
- What would it be if you had to eat the same meal every day for the rest of your life?
- What would you choose—being left alone or being left with your worst enemy on a deserted island?
- The 60s, 70s, 80s, 90s—which decade do you love the most, and why?

Kintsugi Mosaics

There is a practice in Japan called Kintsugi. Instead of throwing away a chipped or broken vase or other ceramic item, it is repaired with lacquer and gold. Kintsugi translates as "golden journey." It restores a broken object in a way that highlights rather than hides the damage. Foundational is the Japanese philosophy of wabi-wabi, which is a belief that there is beauty in imperfections. Analogously, we can find beauty even in the broken parts of ourselves and the difficult things in our lives. We will use broken ceramic pieces to create a beautiful mosaic and sprinkle with gold dust. When you look in this mirror, see yourself differently!

- hand-held mirrors (can be purchased online in bulk)
- china saucers of various patterns or colors (can be found at thrift stores)
- gallon-sized Ziploc bags
- disposable plates
- spackle
- plastic knives or lollypop sticks to spread spackle
- other items like buttons, jewelry, shells, or stones provide added interest

- gold mica powder
- gloves to protect hands from sharp edges

1. Place saucers in a plastic bag (one at a time) and break them by dropping them on a cement surface or gently banging with a hard object.
2. Create a mosaic design by arranging the broken pieces and other items on the intended surface.
3. Take a picture of your arrangement and then move pieces to a plate (loosely maintaining design).
4. Spread the spackle.
5. Press the broken pieces and other items into the spackle to secure them.
6. Sprinkle mica powder (sparingly) on exposed spackle.

Table Talk

- Can you identify a silver lining in a difficult situation you have faced or are currently facing?
- The Bible says, "When I am weak, then I am strong," (2 Corinthians 12:10). Can you give an example of this from your life or the life of someone you know?
- C. S. Lewis said, "God whispers in our pleasures but shouts in our pain."[8] How is God whispering and shouting to you in your life?

Second Series—Journey

Journey

Fun

Give everyone a journal as a welcome gift. You can use composition books, spiral notebooks, or journals purchased online in bulk. Allow guests to make their journal unique by providing markers and stickers to decorate the cover.

Warmly welcome and introduce all guests to one another. Share why you started the group as well as upcoming dates, topics, and projects.

- ♦ Share the circumstances of your birth, including the time of year, place, family, and any special particulars.
- ♦ Describe a snapshot of your life around the age of seven, including who you lived with, what winters were like, and what was a source of warmth in your life.

Journey

We will look at our lives so that we can learn, celebrate, and navigate this journey of life together. Just like travel companions are essential when taking a trip, it is a great idea to process and plan our lives in community. Friends give us eyes to see the beautiful, meaningful, and funny. Different life events, decisions, and circumstances have shaped our lives and brought us to the current moment. Every day presents an opportunity to shape our lives and the lives of those around us. Our stories hold precious treasures for ourselves and others. Our time together is just a jumping-off point to promote thought and discussion, a time to listen to and encourage each other.

Discussion Blueprint

Many analogies have been made to life. For example, life is a roller coaster—sometimes up, sometimes down. Other examples include life being like a dance, an onion, a garden, and/or a puzzle. Is there one you find especially true?

In his very popular book *The Purpose Driven Life*, Rick Warren concludes that life is a test, life is a trust, and life is a temporary assignment.[9]

Pass around a box of chocolates for everyone to take a chocolate.

In the movie *Forest Gump*, Forest Gump's mom famously said, "Life is like a box of chocolates; you never know what you're gonna get."[10] Show the short movie clip; you can find it on YouTube.

Known and Loved

- ◆ Forrest's mother sees her destiny as being his mom. What role do our relationships play in the meaning and purpose of life?
- ◆ How do we balance and come to peace with "what you get" and "what you do with what you get" as we examine our lives up to this point and plan for the future?

Beyond the Table

Ponder the following questions for journaling:

- Who are the people in your life most important to you?
- List all the roles you fulfill, such as mom, aunt, daughter, friend, neighbor, accountant, waitress, volunteer, worshiper, and so on.
- How have your roles changed over time?
- Are there current roles you would like to lean into more/less?

Book Recommendations

- *Man's Search for Meaning*[11] by Victor Frankl
- *Undistracted*[12] by Bob Goff
- *Seeking God*[13] by Trevor Hudson
- *The Purpose Driven Life*[14] by Rick Warren
- *Love Walked Among Us*[15] by Paul Miller

Beautiful Destinations

Mt Otemanu, Bora Bora, Tahiti

Frederiksborg Castle and Gardens, Hillerød, Denmark

Cinque Terre, Italy

Kirkjufell Mountain, Iceland

Kyoto, Japan

Istanbul, Turkey

Lanikai Beach, Oahu, Hawaii

Lake Tahoe, California

Oia Village, Santorini Island, Greece

New York, New York

Ukraine

Trevi Fountain, Rome, Italy

Fun

Place stickers under two plates and give prizes to people who are eating from those plates.

Allow everyone to look at travel pictures, choose, and share the top three pictured places that they would most like to visit.

Known and Heard

- ◆ What problem in the world would you most like to see fixed, or which need would you most like to see met?
- ◆ Name a person you consider having lived or to be living a good life. Why did you choose this person?

Beautiful Destinations

Trips take planning. Our life is an incredible journey, but we often spend more time planning our weekend or a vacation than examining our lives. We tend to reserve the question "What do you want to do or be?" for school-age children or college graduates. We should routinely be asking this fun and exciting question of ourselves. We must evaluate what is important to us, keep an eye on the result, use our time intentionally, and work to make the necessary changes in our lives, even if they are very slow.

Discussion Blueprint

Sharing stories. By sharing our stories and those of others, we can inspire and help each other clarify and examine what is worthy of our time, resources, hopes, and dreams.

Andre Louf was born in Belgium in 1929. He became a monk when he was eighteen, shortly after World War II ended. He was a writer and a spiritual mentor to many and known for his joyful simplicity. He would spend time at the Trappist monastery in Boise, Idaho, each year. After he passed away, his Trappist monk friends wrote the following about him.

A man without boundaries and tenacious in his search for Beauty and its reverberations in reality, he always struck us as a man extraordinarily capable of listening—in the therapeutic quality of which he firmly believed—as a man of potent force of intercession and of fidelity to daily prayer, of incessant ministry of consolation, of penetrating discernment, always ready to spread the mantle of pardon over evil, a man of absolute primacy of mercy… in fraternal relations and towards the facts of life. With respect to the latter, he always warned against giving oneself up to bitterness; he admitted the possibility of moments of sadness that should be welcomed with magnanimity and a smile, nevertheless, and even more, in him was affirmed the ever more acute seeking of the Light, which he found in small daily occurrences and in the persons he met, as traces of the uncreated Light, of the divine Light in which he is finally wrapped. He lived a growing attitude towards a limpid vision of sincerity with regard to himself and to others, of astonishment and wonder towards all creation, in the conviction that the good remains more profound than the most profound evil.[16]

What biographical books or movies have inspired you?

Examples of inspirational movies are *Hacksaw Ridge, Chariots of Fire, Schindler's List, Amazing Grace*.

Known and Loved

Frederick Buechner, an American author and theologian, said, "The place God calls you to is the place where your deep gladness and the world's deep hunger meet."[17]

- ◆ What do you think this means?
- ◆ Do you think this is true? Why or why not?
- ◆ Is there a relationship between our "deep gladness" and our strengths and talents?
- ◆ What sense of calling do you personally have in your life?

Beyond the Table

- Consider your unique skills, talents, and interests. What makes you light up?
- Allow yourself to think and dream of the future!
- Invite God to show you His wonderful plans by carving out some quiet time to pray and listen.

Luggage Tags

Fun

Questions in a Bowl

Copy the questions, cut them apart, fold them, and place them in a bowl. Allow each person to draw a question from the bowl, answer it, and return it to the bowl.

- Did you ever study a foreign language? If so, which one and why did you choose it?
- Where did your family vacation when you were a child?
- Where is the farthest from home you have ever traveled? Where did you go and why?
- What is the best trip you have ever taken? Where did you go and with whom?

Luggage Tags

Create colorful and fun luggage tags! Life is a journey with adventures and discoveries awaiting.

- cardboard—premake templates for tags and plastic
- felt in a variety of colors
- patterned fabrics
- clear plastic
- embroidery thread and needles
- decorative papers
- colored pens or markers

1. Use templates to cut felt and plastic.
2. Use your imagination to decorate the back of the tag with fabric or felt.
3. Sew the plastic window onto the front of the tag.
4. Write identifying information on decorative paper and slip it behind plastic.

Table Talk

- ◆ Have you tried a new food, recipe, or restaurant recently? Share and rate this experience.
- ◆ Where do you like to take out-of-town guests? What do you like to show them when they visit you?
- ◆ Have you discovered the intersection of your talents, strengths, interests, calling, and joy?

Book Recommendation

Go deeper in your journey with God. *Spiritual Classics, Selected Readings on the Twelve Spiritual Disciplines*[18] is a compilation of short excerpts from various authors on twelve spiritual disciplines, including meditation, prayer, fasting, study, simplicity, solitude, submission, service, confession, worship, guidance, and celebration. It includes fifty-two excerpts with commentary by Richard Foster.

Olive wood crosses from Israel

Child of God

Fun

Give everyone a small cross to keep in their pocket as a reminder that they are a child of God and He is always with them.

Known and Heard

- ♦ What is your earliest memory of your mom or dad?
- ♦ Growing up, were you close to any of your grandparents? Tell us about that relationship.
- ♦ Did you have a childhood best friend? Have you remained in contact with them?

Child of God

Many people lack a deeply felt confidence that they are beloved by God. God's love is unshakable, and He has compassion for us that we cannot even imagine. His love for us is fierce and, at the same time, tender. He desires that we be reconciled to Him and experience the peace of His protection and presence each day. A mother's deep love for her child is a mere shadow of God's love for us; it gives us a glimpse of God's love. We are daughters of the King, and that changes everything.

> "Though the mountains be shaken and the hills be removed, yet my unfailing love for you will not be shaken nor my covenant of peace be removed" says the Lord, who has compassion on you. (Isaiah 54:10)

Gustav Klimt's *Mother and Child* (detail from the *Three Ages of Women*)

Discussion Blueprint

Mother and Child by Gustav Klimt. Pass out copies of Gustav Klimt's *Mother and Child* (or show on digital screen). Gustav Klimt was born in Vienna in 1862. He grew up poor and supported his family throughout his life. Early in his career, he specialized in painting the interiors of theaters. He is well known for his use of gold leafing and painting in the Art Nouveau style, which is characterized by a sense of dynamism and movement. He lived with his mother his entire life and died at the age of fifty-five.

Allow a few minutes to observe the artwork.

– Describe the scene in detail. What do you notice?
– What story does the picture tell?
– How does this painting make you feel? Does it evoke memories or desires?
– What does it tell us about the relationship between this mother and child?

Father's Love Letter. The love of the most loving and perfect parent for their children is only a faint reflection of God's overflowing and inexhaustible love for you. It is like the light of a little candle compared to the sun. Give everyone a copy of the Father's Love Letter. The Father's Love Letter is a compilation of true and powerful statements about God's love from the Old and New Testaments of the Bible. Barry Adams wrote the letter in 1999 for a sermon. It has since been translated into 125 languages and shared with millions. You can download and print the letter from the website www.fathersloveletter.com.

Known and Loved

- What is the most important thing you have learned in your lifetime about love?
- What could keep a person from believing that God loves them?
- How did your parents impact your view of God for good or bad?

God feels toward us like a mother feels toward her own dear child. When the child is struggling, falling, even making terrible and hurtful decisions, a mother's heart is full of love. She wants her child to have freedom, peace, and wholeness. (Julian of Norwich)[19]

Beyond the Table

Write 1 John 3:1 on a three-by-five card and memorize it.

> See what kind of love the Father has given to us, that we should be called children of God: and so we are. (1 John 3:1)

The Spirit himself bears witness with our Spirit that we are children of God. (Romans 8:16)

FATHER'S LOVE LETTER

An intimate message from God to you.

My Child,

You may not know me, but I know everything about you. Psalm 139:1 *I know when you sit down and when you rise up.* Psalm 139:2 *I am familiar with all your ways.* Psalm 139:3 *Even the very hairs on your head are numbered.* Matthew 10:29-31 *For you were made in my image.* Genesis 1:27 *In me you live and move and have your being.* Acts 17:28 *For you are my offspring.* Acts 17:28 *I knew you even before you were conceived.* Jeremiah 1:4-5 *I chose you when I planned creation.* Ephesians 1:11-12 *You were not a mistake, for all your days are written in my book.* Psalm 139:15-16 *I determined the exact time of your birth and where you would live.* Acts 17:26 *You are fearfully and wonderfully made.* Psalm 139:14 *I knit you together in your mother's womb.* Psalm 139:13 *And brought you forth on the day you were born.* Psalm 71:6 *I have been misrepresented by those who don't know me.* John 8:41-44 *I am not distant and angry, but am the complete expression of love.* 1 John 4:16 *And it is my desire to lavish my love on you.* 1 John 3:1 *Simply because you are my child and I am your Father.* 1 John 3:1 *I offer you more than your earthly father ever could.* Matthew 7:11 *For I am the perfect father.* Matthew 5:48 *Every good gift that you receive comes from my hand.* James 1:17 *For I am your provider and I meet all your needs.* Matthew 6:31-33 *My plan for your future has always been filled with hope.* Jeremiah 29:11 *Because I love you with an everlasting love.* Jeremiah 31:3 *My thoughts toward you are countless as the sand on the seashore.* Psalm 139:17-18 *And I rejoice over you with singing.* Zephaniah 3:17 *I will never stop doing good to you.* Jeremiah 32:40 *For you are my treasured possession.* Exodus 19:5 *I desire to establish you with all my heart and all my soul.* Jeremiah 32:41 *And I want to show you great and marvelous things.* Jeremiah 33:3 *If you seek me with all your heart, you will find me.* Deuteronomy 4:29 *Delight in me and I will give you the desires of your heart.* Psalm 37:4 *For it is I who gave you those desires.* Philippians 2:13 *I am able to do more for you than you could possibly imagine.* Ephesians 3:20 *For I am your greatest encourager.* 2 Thessalonians 2:16-17 *I am also the Father who comforts you in all your troubles.* 2 Corinthians 1:3-4 *When you are brokenhearted, I am close to you.* Psalm 34:18 *As a shepherd carries a lamb, I have carried you close to my heart.* Isaiah 40:11 *One day I will wipe away every tear from your eyes.* Revelation 21:3-4 *And I'll take away all the pain you have suffered on this earth.* Revelation 21:3-4 *I am your Father, and I love you even as I love my son, Jesus.* John 17:23 *For in Jesus, my love for you is revealed.* John 17:26 *He is the exact representation of my being.* Hebrews 1:3 *He came to demonstrate that I am for you, not against you.* Romans 8:31 *And to tell you that I am not counting your sins.* 2 Corinthians 5:18-19 *Jesus died so that you and I could be reconciled.* 2 Corinthians 5:18-19 *His death was the ultimate expression of my love for you.* 1 John 4:10 *I gave up everything I loved that I might gain your love.* Romans 8:31-32 *If you receive the gift of my son Jesus, you receive me.* 1 John 2:23 *And nothing will ever separate you from my love again.* Romans 8:38-39 *Come home and I'll throw the biggest party heaven has ever seen.* Luke 15:7 *I have always been Father, and will always be Father.* Ephesians 3:14-15
My question is... Will you be my child? John 1:12-13
I am waiting for you. Luke 15:11-32

Love, Your Dad
Almighty God

Father's Love Letter, used by permission Father Heart Communications © 1999,

www.FathersLoveLetter.com

Stories

Fun

Pass the Gift

Wrap a small gift that guests pass around while music is playing. Without looking at the players, stop the music. Eliminate the person holding the gift from the game. Keep playing until one person remains and gets to keep the gift.

Known and Heard

- ◆ Name three characteristics you want to develop in increasing measure (e.g., creativity, peacefulness, playfulness, generosity, listening, kindness, boldness, tenacity, gratefulness).
- ◆ Share one important thing that happened in your life this past week.

Stories

There is great value in learning, remembering, and retelling the stories of those who have gone before us and in sharing our own stories. Sharing stories knits our hearts together, teaches us, and inspires us.

Discussion Blueprint

Ashley's Sack. In 2007, a woman found this sack buried in a pile of material at a flea market and purchased the lot of fabric for twenty dollars.

Show the picture of Ashley's Sack. It reads as follows:

> My great grandmother Rose
> mother of Ashley gave her this sack when
> she was sold at age 9 in South Carolina
> it held a tattered dress 3 handfuls of
> pecans a braid of Roses hair. Told her
> It be filled with my Love always

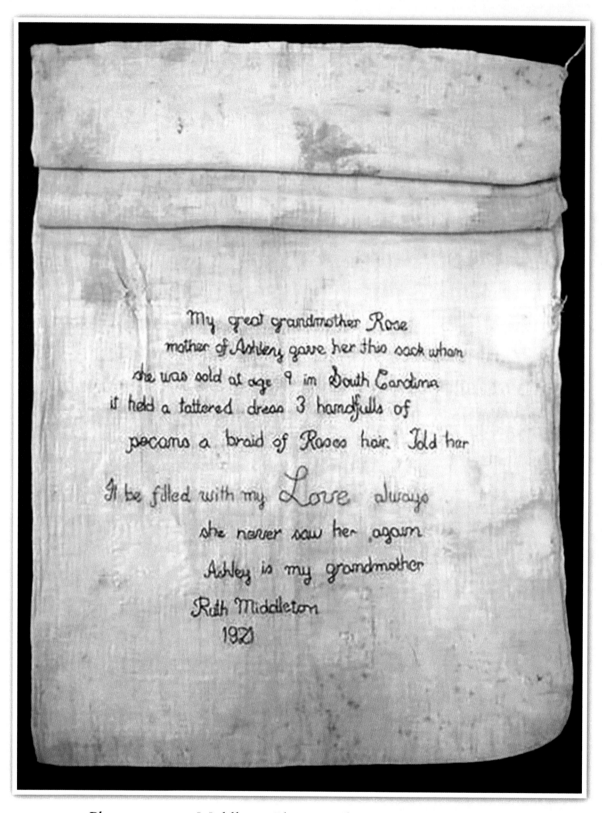

Photo courtesy Middleton Place via Shameran81/Wikimedia

she never saw her again
Ashley is my grandmother
Ruth Middleton

1920

Pause for a moment as people consider the weight of this story.

This sack tells so many stories and held so much meaning for so many people: Rose, who gave it to her daughter; Ashley, the nine-year-old who received it; Ashley's child, who ultimately gave it to Ruth; and Ruth, who embroidered the story on the sack. We don't know its story from there, but we can only imagine it was significant to many more people for the next hundred years until its meaning was lost or forgotten. Ultimately, it found its way into a thrift store.

In addition to the very personal story, the sack tells the story of a time and place in the American South and the cruel practice of slavery.

Upon its discovery, it was donated to Middleton Place, a plantation in South Carolina, and it is currently displayed at the National Museum of African American History and Culture. (To learn more about Ashley's Sack, read *All That She Carried* by Tiya Miles.)

— Do you have any objects or keepsakes from your parents, grandparents, or great-grandparents? Why do you keep them, and what story, or part of a story, do they tell?
— How much do you know about your family's history or the individual stories of your relatives? Are there hard parts? Are there parts correlated with much larger stories, such as war or persecution?

An eternal perspective. Picture a rope so long it wraps around the whole world several times; in fact, it never ends. The first two inches of that rope are colored red. The rope represents our lives into eternity, and the red part represents our time on earth. Most of us don't have an eternal perspective and spend much of our lives only thinking about the red part. We would be wise to live our short lives here on earth with an eternal perspective.[20] How can we cultivate an eternal perspective?

Known and Loved

Sharing Testimonies

Our lives are shaped by so much: the difficult parts, our great loves, opportunities, and ultimately what we make of all these things. How we see the story and trajectory of our lives impacts how we relate to others and what we do with our precious time. Looking back on our lives, we can see the threads God has woven into our stories. We can look to the future with hope and confidence, knowing that God will never leave or forsake us. He is our Father; we can take refuge under His wing.

Before the meeting, ask one or two people to share their testimonies with the group. Telling stories was Jesus's primary way of teaching. The Bible says we will overcome by the blood of the lamb and the word of our testimony.[21] Our stories can remarkably change lives and point people to the Lord as Savior.

Beyond the Table

Think about your story.

– What have been the most meaningful experiences of your life?
– What seasons of trial or pain have you survived?
– How has God provided for you?

> Fellowship is an expression of both love and humility. It springs from a desire to bring benefit to others coupled with a sense of personal weakness and need. It has a double motive: the wish to help and the wish to be helped, the wish to edify and the wish to be edified. (J.I. Packer)[22]

Cairns

Fun

Fun Facts

- A Jewish tradition is to leave a rock at the gravesite when visiting to honor the deceased person.
- In the 1900s, Waldron Bates built cairns to mark trails in Arcadia National Park; these cairns remain there today.
- Cairns, made and used by people worldwide, can be found in Tibet, on the Inca Trail, and in the American west.
- Scottish, Norse, and Celtic people made giant cairns to serve as lighthouses.

Cairns

A cairn is a heap of stones piled to memorialize events, honor people, mark boundaries, or serve as guideposts to lead the way. Creating a physical reminder of events and people is an honored tradition in all cultures and times. Let's make cairns to pay homage to the events and people who have shaped our lives.

- stones in a variety of sizes and colors
- glue guns and glue sticks
- pen and paper for journaling answers to questions

> You can purchase colorful polished stones online in bulk. Pebble tile twelve-inch-by-twelve-inch panels for floors and walls come in various colors and sizes. The stones on these panels are also great for making cairns. You can buy them at home-improvement retail stores.

1. Think about your story.

  - Who have been the most important people in your life?
  - Have you had a notable mentor, friend, or relative who has significantly shaped your life or thinking?
  - What have been the most meaningful experiences of your life?
  - What seasons of trial or pain have you survived?
  - How has God provided for you?

2. Choose your stones to create your cairn. The number of stones and the colors/patterns can help tell the story. Your cairn can represent a season in your life, a life-changing event, special people in your life, or a combination.

3. Use your cairn as a reminder of God's mighty working and provision in your life.

> In the book of Joshua, God commanded the Israelites to take twelve stones from the Jordan to commemorate His rescue of them by parting the Jordan River. God told them in times to come, when children ask their fathers what the rocks mean, they should be told the story of the great crossing and how God dried up the water so that they could pass "so that all the peoples of the earth may know that the hand of the Lord is mighty, that you may fear the Lord God forever" (Joshua 4:24).

Table Talk

Share the story of your cairn.

Holiday, Seasonal, and Special Gatherings

Valentine's Day

Fun

Splashes of pink, red, and white, conversation hearts, heart lollipops, and a warm greeting will set the tone for a fun Valentine's celebration.

Known and Heard

♦ What are your favorite romantic movies or books?

♦ Did you ever receive or write a love letter?

♦ Does your family, extended family, or friend circle have epic love stories (e.g., fifty-plus years of marriage or a story of great sacrifice, forgiveness, or overcoming)?

Felt Heart Garland

This is a simple craft that will allow for lots of conversation and a chance to celebrate love and friendship during the coldest time of the year.

• squares of felt in shades of pink, red, purple, and blues

• string

• small pompoms

• scissors

• glue guns

• cardboard—precut heart templates in various sizes

1. Design your garland.

2. Cut hearts using the heart templates.

3. String together.

Table Talk

Dr. Gary Chapman wrote a best-selling book, The Five Love Languages.[23] He believes people show and receive love primarily in five ways:

— words of affirmation

— spending quality time together

— giving gifts

— performing acts of service

— physical touch

These ways of showing and receiving love are relevant to relationships with family and friends, not just romantic relationships.

Known and Loved

- Which of the five love languages best describes your primary love language?
- How can "speaking different love languages" create problems in a relationship?
- Looking back on your childhood, how did your parents or primary caregiver express love? What impact did that have on how you receive or communicate love?
- The greatest love story is God's love for us. How can you discover and experience His love for you in a more profound way?

If you have not previously given out copies of the Father's Love Letter (Child of God Huddle, page 42), do so now.

Beyond the Table

Contemplate your love language and the love language of those you live with and love. Experiment with expressing love by using the love languages you are less comfortable with. Deliberately show love in the way it will be best received by those you love.

> So we have come to know and to believe the love that God has for us. God is love, and whoever abides in love abides in God, and God abides in him. (1 John 4:16)

Easter

Fun

- To celebrate spring, give everyone a small plant or flower.
- Set out hardboiled eggs, rubber bands, and egg dyes; let everyone make a tie-dyed egg.
- Serve pancakes and tell the story of Shrove Tuesday. Pancakes are traditionally eaten on Shrove Tuesday, the day before Ash Wednesday. People ate pancakes to use up the eggs, fats, and milk in the house (rich foods they would abstain from during Lent.) In 1445, in England, a tradition of pancake racing began. Legend has it that a woman lost track of time on Shrove Tuesday because she was busy cooking pancakes in her kitchen. Suddenly, she heard the church bells ringing to call everyone to the church for confession. She raced out of her home and ran to church, holding her frying pan and wearing her apron. Today's pancake races have strict rules, such as tossing the pancake at the beginning and end, and participants dress in their Sunday best.

Known and Heard

Lent is a season of reflection and preparation before Easter. Traditionally, people fast from certain kinds of food.

- What other things could you do to make this time meaningful?

The following are ideas of things to reduce: criticism, judgment, complaining, people pleasing, anxious thoughts, harmful habits.

The following are ideas of things to increase: time for reflection, gratitude, rest, prayer, feeding birds, planting flowers.

Easter

Easter is the most important holiday on the Christian calendar. Jesus conquered death on our behalf and made a way for us to live in heaven with Him for eternity. On Easter, we celebrate new life and new beginnings.

Small diorama in peat pot

Discussion Blueprint

The donkey and chick are two animals that point to Jesus's heart.

Donkey. A week before the Last Supper, Jesus traveled to Jerusalem from Bethany and rode into town on a young, borrowed donkey. Jerusalem was very crowded, and people greeted him by throwing their cloaks and palm branches in His path and saying, "Hosanna," which means "Save us." He did not arrive with a royal entourage in a golden chariot drawn by beautiful horses but on an ordinary, humble donkey. He did not go to a palace but to the Temple because He was a spiritual, not political, king. Jesus showed humility and great compassion throughout His life; He touched the "untouchables," healed the sick, washed His disciples' feet, laughed with children, cried with those who were sad, and raised the dead.

Chick. We know that a week after He arrived in Jerusalem to the cries of "Save us," the same crowd would shout, "Crucify him." Jesus knew that although they greeted Him as a king, many would reject Him. This caused Him great sadness; as He looked out over the city, He said,

> O Jerusalem, Jerusalem, the city that kills the prophets and stones those who are sent to it! How often would I have gathered your children together as a hen gathers her brood under her wings, and you were not willing! (Matthew 23:37)

Despite their impending rejection of Him, His heart was for them; He was not angry, bitter, or indifferent to them; He wept for them and desired to "gather them as a hen gathers her brood under her wing." He compares himself to a protective mother. Think of a hen when a predator approaches; they swell with anger and courage; they stand their ground. They will die if they must, their children tucked securely beneath their soft bodies.

God is many things: holy, righteous, just, omnipresent, and powerful. But let Jesus's riding into Jerusalem on a donkey and comparing Himself to a mother hen remind us of a side of God that we may need to remember: He is humble, gentle, loving, sheltering, fiercely protective, and sacrificial. He is the awaited Messiah. He died on the cross so those who turn from their sins, accept, and follow Him, can have eternal life with Him and God the Father.

Known and Loved

- About Jesus, T.R. Glover said, "Men may love him or hate him, but they do it intensely."[24] Do you think this statement is true, and if so, why?
- Have your beliefs about Easter changed your life? If so, how?

Beyond the Table

Go into the world in peace and joy, with gratitude, knowing you are loved. If Jesus is your Savior, your eternity is secure! Follow up individually with anyone who may have questions and be a resource on their faith journey.

> The gospel is not good advice to men but good news about Christ; not an invitation to us to do anything but a declaration of what God has done; not a demand but an offer. (John Stott) [25]

Summer Herb Gardens

Fun

- Welcome your guests with summer classics like lemonade and watermelon. Set the tone with a summer vacation playlist. If the weather permits, set up outside.
- Invite those who are comfortable to take their shoes off, walk in the grass, and work barefoot. Research links walking barefoot on the earth with reduced inflammation, increased wound healing, and improved sleep.[26] Many people believe it is akin to clean air and water, nutritious food, and physical activity.
- Barefoot or not, being together is good for your health! Scientific evidence proves that healthy friendships are crucial for well-being and longevity.[27]

Herb Gardens with Markers

Playing with dirt brings out the kid in all of us. The miracle of watching a plant grow from a seed gives us hope for the future. Fresh herbs enhance the flavor of food and are good for you.

- tin planters (can be purchased online in bulk or at dollar stores)
- garden soil
- small rocks or gravel
- herb seeds like basil, marjoram, chives, oregano, thyme, or sage (or seedlings)
- large popsicle sticks
- flat pebbles
- paint markers
- glue guns and glue sticks

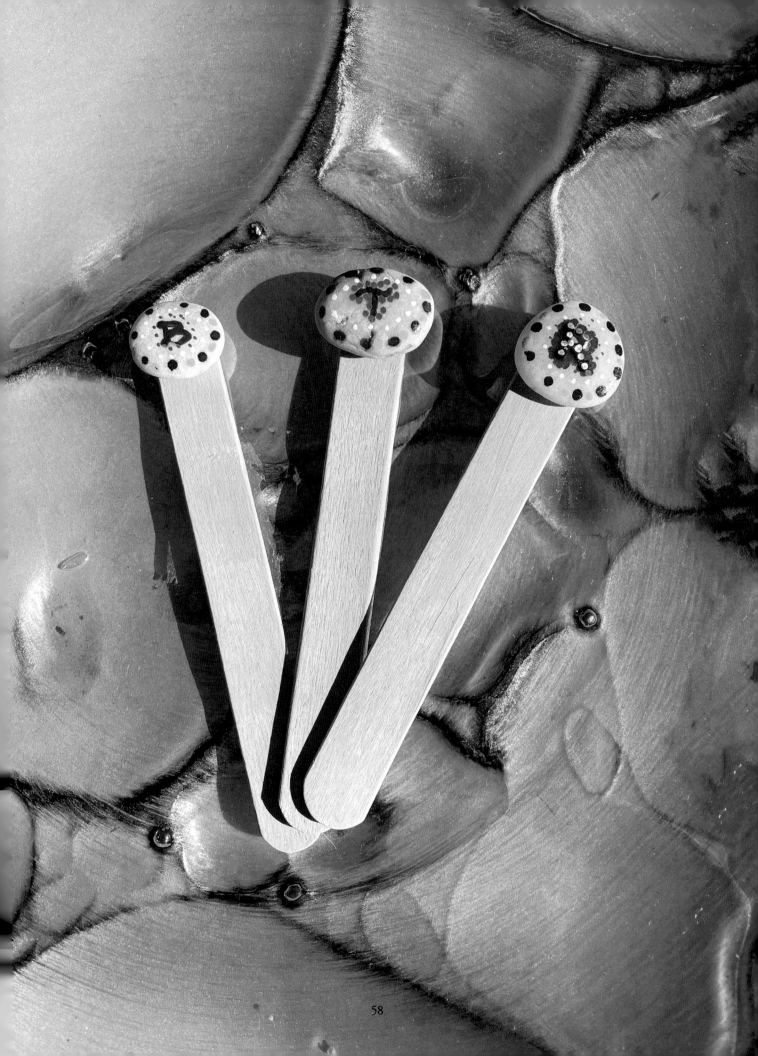

1. Fill the bottom of the planter with two inches of gravel for drainage.
2. Fill the planter with soil two inches below the top.
3. Plant seeds and water.
4. Write the name of herbs planted or other identifying information on small stones and glue them onto a popsicle stick.

Table Talk

- What was an unexpected joy this past year?
- Name three things you are very grateful for right now.
- Name something that would make you smile if it happened in the next five years.

Fall Sweater Pumpkins

Fun

- Put Epsom salt in small cellophane gift bags and tie them with fall-colored ribbons to give to your friends. Include a note:

  > With warmest wishes for your well-being.
  > Enjoy the simple pleasure of a hot bath.
  > Epson salt, rich in magnesium and sulfate,
  > soothes tired muscles and promotes relaxation.

- Remind everyone of the importance of self-care during the dark winter months.

Some ideas: aromatic candles, soothing music, hot drinks in favorite mugs, long baths, calling a friend, short walk outside, journaling.

Sweater Pumpkins

These playful pumpkins will add cozy charm to your fall decor. They are easy to make and can be embellished to add individual style and flair.

- foam pumpkins that can be carved, 5.5" x 4.5" (spray paint white)
- old sweaters (precut into pieces to cover pumpkins)
- jute ribbon
- raffia
- felt
- embellishments like costume jewelry and buttons
- scissors
- glue guns and glue sticks
- X-Acto knife or paring knife

1. Cut the stem out of the pumpkin.

2. Wrap the pumpkin with a sweater. Depending on the sweater, each sleeve may be able to cover one pumpkin, as well as the front and back panels. Glue the sweater on the bottom (if you used the sleeve) and into the stem hole.

3. Use jute ribbon to create a stem, and embellish with felt leaves, raffia, jewelry, and so on.

Table Talk

- Who is always there for you and listens to you? How do you feel about them?
- Give a recent example of how you have used your time and talent to help someone in a small or big way.

Beyond the Table

Give everyone an acorn and a copy of Jeremiah 17:7–8 to meditate on as a reminder that those who trust in the Lord are blessed.

> Blessed is the man who trusts in the Lord, whose trust is in the Lord. He is like a tree planted by water, that sends out its roots by the stream, and does not fear when heat comes, for its leaves remain green, and is not anxious in the year of drought, for it does not cease to bear fruit. (Jeremiah 17:7–8)

Christmas Wreaths

Fun

- Give floating candle gifts to your guests. Make them by placing a three-inch wide floating candle, fresh greens, and cranberries into a small fishbowl. Wrap with white tissue paper and red ribbon. Include a note:

> With warmest wishes for a Merry Christmas.
> Fill with water, light the candle, and enjoy!
> Jesus said, "I am the light of the world.
> Whoever follows me will not walk in darkness,
> but will have the light of life"
> (John 4:14).

- Nativity display. Invite guests who have a favorite or special nativity set to bring it and share why it is special to them.

Wreaths

Christmas wreaths serve as reminders of the deeper meaning of the holiday season, including hope, renewal, and the welcoming of love and joy into our homes. The circular shape symbolizes eternity and God's unending love for us, and the evergreens represent life and hope even during dark seasons.

- twelve-inch to fourteen-inch wreath forms (can be purchased from a dollar store)
- mix of evergreens
- pine cones, berries, ribbons, bows, and other decorations
- green florist wire
- wire cutters (ask guests to bring, as each person will need them)

1. Make twelve to fifteen small bouquets with the evergreens.
2. Wrap bouquets tightly with florist wire and clip wire.
3. Secure wire on the wreath frame to wrap and secure the bouquets. Do not cut the wire you will be wrapping with until you are finished wrapping.
4. Place the bouquet on top of the secured wire and wrap the wire around the stem of the bouquet several times (feeding it between the frame of the wreath).
5. Place the next bouquet below and attach it to the wire.
6. Continue to attach the bouquets and add pine cones, berries, and other decorations as desired.
7. After adding the final bouquet, secure the wire in the back by wrapping it several times around the frame's back.
8. Add a second wire for hanging.

Table Talk

- What is your best Christmas memory from childhood?
- What is your favorite Christmas tradition?
- Many animals hibernate in winter. How can you create time and space for rest, peace, and reflection during the upcoming busy holiday season?

Before everyone leaves, consider singing a Christmas carol together (you can sing a well-known carol or preprint the words).

Beyond the Table

Invite friends to a local Christmas concert to celebrate the season.

Charity Swap

Fun

Purchase bath bombs or a flat of flowers. Wrap individually with colorful tissue paper and a fabric bow. Include a personal note to each friend.

Charity Swap

A charity swap is a great way to impact the world for good. Invite everyone to drop off clothes, jewelry, and household items that they no longer use a few days before your event. Organize items to make shopping easy. Choose a charity to support and put a basket out for donations. Invite everyone to "shop" and make donations in any amount. Highlight the work of the selected charity. Donate all "unsold" items to a local thrift shop. Working together to help others strengthens the bonds of friendship by adding a meaningful and enduring connection.

1. If you were given $25 million to make the world a better place, how would you spend it?
2. Tell us about a generous person you know.

Discussion Blueprint

Discuss the following quotes and verses:

> The greatness of a community is most accurately measured by the compassionate actions of its members. (Coretta Scott King) [28]

> By this we know love, that he laid down his life for us, and we ought to lay down our lives for the brothers. But if anyone has the world's goods and sees his brother in need, yet closes his heart against him, how does God's love abide in him? Little children, let us not love in word or talk but in deed and in truth. (1 John 3:16–18)

> Love begins at home, and it is not how much we do, but how much love we put in the action that we do. (Mother Teresa) [29]

> In all things I have shown you that by working hard in this way we must help the weak and remember the words of the Lord Jesus, how he himself said, "It is more blessed to give than to receive." (Acts 20:35)

Beyond the Table

Continue to clean out closets and drawers and donate to charity regularly.

Book Recommendation

Tattoos on the Heart by Gregory Boyle is the true story of the birth of Homeboy Industries, a ministry to former gang members in Los Angeles, California. [30] It is eye-opening and perspective changing.

Excursions

Consider planning an excursion to have fun, create memories, and allow group members to connect one-on-one. You may be surprised at how many wonderful places are close to home. Let the adventure begin! (Ideas: lunch at a great restaurant, hiking, or visiting a local museum, formal garden, or zoo.)

Feed Them

Sharing food helps people feel welcomed and loved. You don't have to spend much money or time in the kitchen to make delicious food, nourishing to body and soul. Unless you love to cook, keep it simple. The following improvisational "no-recipe" recipes can serve any number of guests. They are easy, fresh, healthy, and fun. An oatmeal or pancake bar and coffee are great for groups that meet in the morning. A big salad, sandwiches, or a baked potato bar are great for lunch. Consider serving a fun drink or dessert if your group meets in the evening.

Salads

Spinach Salad

- spinach
- bacon bits
- red onion
- croutons
- strawberries
- hard-boiled eggs
- mozzarella grated cheese
- poppy seed salad dressing

Greek Salad

- romaine
- red onion
- feta cheese
- olives
- cucumber
- carrot
- tomato
- Greek salad dressing

Thai Salad

- shredded coleslaw mix or shredded purple cabbage and shredded carrots
- mandarin oranges
- cucumber
- red bell pepper
- peanuts
- wonton strips
- shelled edamame
- Thai salad dressing

Winter Salad

- field greens
- goat cheese
- red onion (sautéed five to seven minutes in hot butter or oil)
- dried cranberries
- candied pecans
- croutons
- balsamic salad dressing

Your mind will always believe everything
you tell it. Feed it faith. Feed it truth.
Feed it with love.
-Anon.

Orzo Salad

- arugula
- orzo pasta
- canned corn (drain)
- bruschetta (don't drain)
- sunflower seeds
- dried cranberries
- shredded mozzarella
- ranch dressing

Fall Salad

- kale
- sliced apples or pears
- roasted butternut squash
- walnuts
- dried cranberries
- croutons
- cider vinaigrette dressing

Cobb Salad

- romaine
- red onion
- crumbled blue cheese
- hard-boiled egg
- avocado
- crispy bacon bits
- cherry tomatoes
- vinaigrette dressing

Quinoa Salad

- tricolored quinoa
- diced peppers
- chickpeas
- cucumbers
- pistachios
- red onion
- coarsely chopped lacinato kale
- dressing for kale—equal parts water, sesame oil, and lemon juice (add some salt)

Sandwiches

Grilled Cheese

- loaf of white or sourdough bread
- cheddar and American cheese
- butter
- served with tomato soup

Old Continent

- French baguettes
- thinly sliced deli ham
- Cooper sharp cheese
- served with apple slices

Turkey Rachel

- rye bread
- turkey
- Swiss cheese
- coleslaw
- Russian or thousand island dressing

Gobbler

- rolls
- turkey
- stuffing
- cranberry sauce

Barbecue Chicken

- Hawaiian rolls
- chicken breasts (cook for several hours in a crockpot, shred with a fork, add sauce, and return to crockpot)
- barbecue sauce
- cheddar cheese slices
- served with crudités like carrots, celery, or peppers and ranch dressing

Topping Bars

Pancake Bar

- pancakes (use protein pancake mix)
- choose several of the following add-ins or toppings:
  - butter
  - maple syrup
  - confectioner's sugar
  - bananas
  - berries—strawberries, blueberries, raspberries
  - chocolate chips
  - raspberry jam

Oatmeal Bar

- oatmeal (use steel cut oatmeal)
- choose several of the following toppings:
  - berries—strawberries, blueberries, raspberries
  - bananas
  - chopped nuts—pecans, almonds, or walnuts
  - mini chocolate chips
  - cinnamon
  - seeds—flax or chia

Baked Potato Bar

- baked potatoes (use 8-10 ounce scrubbed russet potatoes)
- choose several of the following toppings:
  - sour cream
  - butter
  - shredded cheddar
  - bacon bits

- black beans
- salsa
- chives
- steamed broccoli
- ranch

Tips for Baking Potatoes

- Heat oven to 450 degrees Fahrenheit.
- Poke potatoes with a fork.
- Bake for twenty-five minutes.
- Brush with melted butter or oil and salt.
- Bake for an additional twenty minutes.
- Cut, squeeze, fluff, and serve.

Drinks

Root Beer Floats

- root beer (offer regular and diet)
- vanilla ice cream
- served with soft or hard pretzels

Party Punch

- ginger ale
- pineapple juice
- frozen strawberries in sugar

Dessert Punch

- Fresca
- cranberry juice
- rainbow sherbet

Mexican Hot Chocolate

- warmed milk
- cocoa
- sugar
- cayenne pepper (pinch)

Ginger Tea

- green tea
- fresh slices of ginger
- lemon
- honey

Haldi Doodh—Indian Turmeric Milk

- warmed milk
- turmeric
- cinnamon
- ginger

Conclusion

Huddles build bridges to the church. In Tim Keller's last published article, he urged Christians to find informational and positive ways, outside of ordinary church, to expose people to Christianity, create places and spaces to point others to the Lord, and to respond to doubt and different opinions with humility and thoughtfulness.[31] Huddles are just that. I hope and pray that by building authentic community, you will have many opportunities to share the joy and hope found in Jesus. Your huddle is a seed-scattering ministry of hospitality to work closely with and complement the vital work of the local church. As people desire to learn and grow in Christian faith, invite them to church and Bible study, pray with and for them, find ways to serve together, and continue to share life.

Acknowledgments

Thank You, Lord, for giving me this good work to do, helping me walk in it, and giving me glimpses of Your miraculous movement. To Amy, serving shoulder-to-shoulder with you is a source of joy and strength. Janet, Donna, Teresa, Karin, and Lisa, your love and leadership are reaping eternal rewards. Danelle, your joie de vivre and beautiful photography add immense spark and beauty. Kiley, thank you for your help over the summer of 2022. Joan and Christine, your partnership in prayer is powerful, priceless, and appreciated beyond measure. Ryan and Jay, your financial partnership reflects your belief in me and this ministry, which fuels and sustains my ardor. Ryan, the publishing of this book was made possible by your extreme generosity and huge heart. Your love, kindness, and generosity inspire me and deeply touch my heart. Each member of each huddle is a treasure and delight to me. Together, you advanced the creation of this book, and I am profoundly appreciative.

About the Author

Sherri DeWalt has been dedicated to connecting, encouraging, and teaching women to grow in their relationship with God and others for more than twenty years. Her home, a hub of creativity and conversation, welcomes new and old friends alike, fostering an environment of shared life and community. In addition to her impactful work with women, she is a passionate attorney focused on justice and humanitarian issues. Sherri is happily married, has two grown children, and enjoys the company of her beloved dog. She and her family reside just outside of Philadelphia, Pennsylvania.

Bibliography

Abrams, Zara. "The Science of Why Friendships Keep Us Healthy." *American Psychological Association* (June 1, 2023). https://www.apa.org/monitor/2023/06/cover-story-science-friendship.

Adams, Barry. "Father's Love Letter." *Father Heart Communications* (1999). https://www.fathersloveletter.com/media center.html.

Alcorn, Randy. *It's All about Jesus*. Eugene, OR: Harvest House Publishers, 2022.

Allen, Summer. "Eight Reasons Why Awe Makes Your Life Better." *Greater Good Magazine* (September 26, 2018). https://greatergood.berkeley.edu/article/item/eight_reasons_why_awe_makes_your_life_better.

Boyle, Fr. Gregory, *Tattoos on the Heart*. New York: Simon & Schuster, 2010.

Brown, Joshua, and Joel Wong. "How Gratitude Changes You and Your Brain." *Greater Good Magazine*, (June 6, 2017). https://greatergood.berkeley.edu/article/item/how_gratitude_changes_you_and_your_brain.

Bruess, Carol. "Do You Know the 5 Love Languages? Here's What They Are-and How to Use Them." TED, (February 8, 202). https://ideas.ted.com/whats-your-favorite-persons-love-language-heres-how-to-tell-and-how-to-use-it/.

Butterfield, Rosaria. *The Gospel Comes with a House Key*. Wheaton, Illinois: Crossway, 2018.

Butterfield, Rosaria, "Ten Things You Should Know About Christian

Hospitality." Crossway, (April 8, 2018). https://www.crossway.org/articles/10-things-you-should-know-about-christian-hospitality/.

Chan, Francis. "Rope Illustration." YouTube video clip, https://youtu.be/86dsfBbZfWs?si=LMUKmUjVNJ3viJmQ.

Chapman, Gary. *The Five Love Languages*. Farmington Hills, MI: Walker Large Print, 2010.

Foster, Richard, Emilie Griffin. *Spiritual Classics Selected Readings on the Twelve Spiritual Disciplines*. San Francisco: Harper One, 2000.

Fox, Jane. *Conversation Art Cards*. Orlando, FL: Cru Press, 2019.

Frankl, Victor. *Man's Search for Meaning*. Boston: Beacon Press, 2006.

Goff, Bob. *Undistracted*. Nashville, TN: Nelson Books, 2022.

Hassani, Nadia. "How to Make a Basic Terrarium." *The Spruce, Make Your Best Home*. https://www.thespruce.com/how-to-make-terrariums-848007.

Hudson, Trevor. *Finding Another Kind of Life with St. Ignatius and Dallas Willard*. Colorado Springs, CO: NavPress, 2022.

Kelleher, Katy. "Why Do People Stack Stones in the Wild?" *National Geographic*. https://www.nationalgeographic.com/culture/article/why-people-stacks-stones-and-where-to-see-them-in-the-wild

Keller, Timothy, "Lemonade on the Porch (part I): The Gospel in a Post-Christendom Society." *Life in the Gospel*, (Spring 2023), https://gospelinlife.com/article/gospel-in-a-post-christendom-society/.

Kotera, Y., Fido, D. "Effects of Shinrin-Yoku Retreat on Mental Health: a Pilot Study in Fukushima, Japan. *International Journal of Mental Health Addiction*, Vol. 20, pgs. 2652–2664 (2022). https://doi.org/10.1007/s11469-021-00538-7.

Kramer, Laurance. "How to Listen and Enjoy Classical Music." *Psych*, (March 29, 2024). https://psyche.co/guides/how-to-listen-to-classical-music-with-an-open-mind.

Los Angeles Times, "Kings Widow Urges Acts of Compassion," January 17, 2000. https://www.latimes.com/archives/la-xpm-2000-jan-17-mn-54832-story.html.

Miles, Tiya. *All That She Carried*. New York: Random House, 2022.

Miller, Paul. *Love Walked Among Us*. Colorado Springs, CO: NavPress, 2001.

McLaughlin, Rebecca. *Confronting Christianity - 12 Hard Questions for the World's Largest Religion*. Wheaton, IL: Crossway, 2019.

Newman, Kira. "Why Your Friends Are More Important Than You Think." *Greater Good Magazine*, (July 7, 2020). https://greatergood.berkeley.edu/article/item/why_your_friends_are_more_important_than_you_think.

Oschman, James, Gaetan Chevalier, Richard Brown. "The Effects of Grounding (Earthing) on Inflammation, the Immune Response, Wound Healing, and Prevention and Treatment of Chronic Inflammatory and Autoimmune Diseases." *National Library of Medicine*, (March 24, 2015). https://www.ncbi.nlm.nih.gov/pmc/articles/PMC4378297/.

Piper, John. *Don't Waste Your Life*. Wheaton, Illinois: Crossway Books, 2003.

Piper, John. "Don't Waste Your Life." Desiring God, 2003. Video, https://www.desiringgod.org/messages/boasting-only-in-the-cross/excerpts/dont-waste-your-life.

Schaffer, Vikki, et al. "Awe: A Systematic Review within a Cognitive Behavioural Framework and Proposed Cognitive Behavioural Model of Awe." *International Journal of Applied Positive Psychology*, Volume 9, pgs. 101-136, 2023. https://doi.org/10.1007/s41042-023-00116-3.

Schwatzberg, L. (Director). *The Wings of Life* [Film]. 2013, Disneynature. Disney.

Sistine Chapel, "The Creation of Adam." Sistine Chapel. https://www.thesistinechapel.org/the-creation-of-adam.

Steindl-Rast, David, Louis Schwatzberg, (Director). "Gratitude," Grateful Living, 2011, https://grateful.org/resource/gratitude-a-film/.

Truth, Sojourner. *Narrative of Sojourner Truth.* Smyrna, GA: Prestwick House, 2007.

Voskamp, Ann. *One Thousand Gifts.* Grand Rapids, MI: Zondervan, 2010.

Warren, Rick. *The Purpose Driven Life.* Grand Rapids, MI: Zondervan, 2002.

Endnotes

1. Yasuhiro Kotera and Dean Fido, "Effects of Shinrin-Yoku Retreat on Mental Health: a Pilot Study in Fukushima, Japan," *International Journal of Mental Health and Addiction* 20 (2022): 2652–2664, https://doi.org/10.1007/s11469-021-00538-7.

2. Vikki Schaffer, Tyrone Huckstepp, and Lee Kannis-Dymand, "Awe: A Systematic Review within a Cognitive Behavioural Framework and Proposed Cognitive Behavioural Model of Awe," *International Journal of Applied Positive Psychology,* http://doi.org/10.1007/s41042-023-001163.

3. Hans Urs von Balthasar, *Glory of the Lord VOL 1: Seeing the Form* (London: A&C Black, 1982), 18.

4. Joshua Brown and Joel Wong, "How Gratitude Changes You and Your Brain," *Greater Good Magazine*, June 2017, 6. https://greatergood.berkeley.edu/article/item/how_gratitude_changes_you_and_your_brain

5. William Blake, "Auguries of Innocence." *Poets of the English Language* (New York: Viking Press, 1950), Poetry Foundation, https://www.poetryfoundation.org/poems/43650/auguries-of-innocence.

6. Jane Fox, *Conversation Art Cards* (Orlando: Cru Press, 2019).

7. A. W. Tozer, *The Knowledge of the Holy* (New York: Harper Collins, 1978),1.

8. C.S. Lewis, *The Problem of Pain* (New York: Harper Collins 2001), 89-91.

9. Rick Warren, *The Purpose Driven Life*, (Grand Rapids, MI: Zondervan, 2002), 45-54.

10. *Forrest Gump*, directed by Robert Zemeckis (1994, USA: Paramount Pictures). "Life is a Box of Chocolates Scene." Movieclips, https://www.youtube.com/watch?v=m6rXRAmaQiE&t=11s.

11. Victor Frankl, *Man's Search for Meaning* (Boston: Beacon Press, 2006).

12. Bob Goff, *Undistracted* (Nashville, TN: Nelson Books, 2022).

13. Trevor Hudson, *Finding Another Kind of Life with St. Ignatius and Dallas Willard* (Colorado Springs, CO: NavPress, 2022).

14. Rick Warren, *The Purpose Driven Life* (Grand Rapids, MI: Zondervan, 2002).

15. Paul Miller, *Love Walked Among Us*, (Colorado Springs, CO: NavPress, 2001).

16. "Father André Louf has passed from this world to the Father," Monastero di Bose, July 13, 2010, https://www.monasterodibose.it/en/community/news/friends-in-the-everlasting-light/5078-father-andre-louf-has-passed-from-this-world-to-the-father.

17. Frederick Buechner, *Wishful Thinking, A Seeker's ABC's,* (New York: Harper and Row, 1973).

18. Richard Foster and Emilie Griffin, *Spiritual Classics Selected Readings on the Twelve Spiritual Disciplines.* (San Francisco: Harper One, 2000).

19. Julian of Norwich, *Revelations of Divine Love recorded by Julian of Norwich,* Anchoress at Norwich, trans. Grace Warrack, (London, England:1901; Project Gutenberg Ebook, September 2, 2016) LXI, https://www.gutenberg.org/files/52958.

20. Francis Chan, "Rope Illustration," YouTube video, https://youtu.be/86dsfBbZfWs?si=LMUKmUjVNJ3viJmQ.

21. Revelation 12:11

22. J. I. Packer, *God's Words: Studies of Key Bible Themes* (Grand Rapids, MI: Baker Book House, 1981).

23. Gary Chapman, *The Five Love Languages.* (Farmington Hills, MI: Walker Large Print, 2010).

24. Randy Alcorn, *It's All About Jesus,* (Eugene, OR: Harvest House Publishers, 2022), 85.

25. Ib., 102.

26. James Oschman, Gaetan Chevalier, Richard Brown. "The Effects of Grounding (Earthing) on Inflammation, the Immune Response, Wound Healing, and Prevention and Treatment of Chronic Inflammatory and Autoimmune Diseases," *National Library of Medicine,* (March 24 2015), https://www.ncbi.nlm.nih.gov/pmc/articles/PMC4378297/.

27. Zara Abrams. "The Science of Why Friendships Keep Us Healthy." *The American Psychological Association*, (June 1, 2023), hhtp://www.apa.org/monitor/2023/06/cover-story-science-friendship.

28. "King's Widow Urges Acts of Compassion," *Los Angeles Times*, January 17, 2000, https://www.latimes.com/archives/la-xpm-2000-jan-17-mn-54832-story.html.

29. Mother Teresa, "Mother Teresa Nobel Lecture," The Nobel Prize, December 11, 1979, https://www.nobelprize.org/prizes/peace/1979/teresa/lecture/.

30. Gregory Boyle, *Tattoos on the Heart,* (New York: Simon & Schuster, 2011).

31. Timothy Keller, "Lemonade on the Porch (part I): The Gospel in a Post-Christendom Society." *Life in the Gospel*, Spring 2023, https://gospelinlife.com/article/gospel-in-a-post-christendom-society/.

Printed in the United States
by Baker & Taylor Publisher Services